THE TALE TERRIERS / SOMERSET CAT

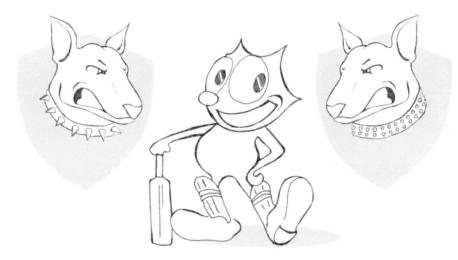

The scrap for cricket's County
Championship 2016 between
Middlesex & Somerset & Yorkshire

by Tim Cawkwell
Sforzinda Books, Norwich, UK

set in Book Antiqua 10 pt

CONTENTS

1 PROLOGUE: GET YOU DOWN TO TAUNTON TOWN

Seasons are integral to our lives. Growth comes with wet and warm, declines with cold. Humans long ago jettisoned hibernation, but spiritually we quicken with the advent of green. What is more, calendars and cycles govern our private lives and our national life. Once upon a time in England, the football season ended and the cricket season began, then it ended and we went back to football. Football is not like that anymore, but nor is international cricket since television and the internet bring this cricket to us throughout the year. One thing still holds to an old pattern – the cricket County Championship. It has changed since it started in the nineteenth century, and changes continue to be made to its structure. Thanks to the weather, however, it starts in April and ends in September, and until the weather changes, the cricket season in England is not going to change. Somewhere in the long future there may be matches played on grounds covered over by a roof, and thus winter cricket, but they are not here yet. At the core of its staying power in England is the place the County Championship provides for long-form cricket, as subtle and elegant an invention of the sporting mind as could be imagined. Sporting thrills take many forms but long-form cricketing thrills are both various and profound, arising as they do from a bedrock of inaction between innings, between overs, between balls. The thrill can be powerful in a crunching boundary, in the stumps being splayed, in a catch at full stretch, in a brilliant run out (the most exciting thing to witness on a sports field?), yet it can also be subtle, for example in the finessed nurdle to square leg, in the ball spinning past the edge of the bat, in a tail-ender defying the best bowler. As it turned out, 2016 was a vintage year for the County Championship, a vintage given nose and body by the fact that its thrilling conclusion coincided with proposals from the England and Wales Cricket Board that, if not taken forward with finesse, could damage future vintages. Were we witnessing the last great year? A new Twenty20 competition is to come into being in the next few years possibly to be called the Super Charge. It has the lofty aim of making cricket more attractive to the young; and the more banal one of bringing in more money to the game. Yet unintended consequences will result as well, chief of which may be the further side-lining of county cricket, perceived as the preserve of the unlucrative and the old and old-fashioned. A particular risk is in the privileging of city-based Test grounds as the places where all this blast cricket takes place, a move that will corkscrew the soul of cricket, a game which is so rural in its origins.

* * *

Cometh April showers at the beginning of the 2016 season, my mind did not turn to cricket and money, but cricket and pure pleasure. Where could I watch it in three dimensions and the fourth one of time? Where could I see living cricketing skill? I live in Norwich, and if one were seeking a starting-point to visit the county grounds, do not start from there. But there were ways round this. A big family holiday was scheduled for August in Porlock in Somerset and once this was fixed, Taunton County Ground began to beckon. 'Get you down to Taunton, old man.'

On Thursday 4th August 2016, I had answered the call and turned up at the county ground to watch Somerset play Durham. Was this just a routine fixture? If so, then this was of no concern to me. One or two of the players involved were an attraction; it would be an even greater pleasure to encounter players unknown to me, like exploring an undiscovered country full of beauteous trees and hills. Being in Taunton itself would be a pleasure for Somerset Cricket Club embodies an essence that to one of the most urbanised countries in the world supplies a vital sliver of rusticity, not just a greensward ruled by Father Time, but a greensward surrounded by fields, hills and rivers.

Like so many cricket grounds in England it is not the product of a grand design but an agglomeration of buildings and structures,

each with its idiosyncrasies. Take the Somerset pavilion at the southern end of the ground.

This has three storeys on one side to give spectators a view above the bowler's arm, and a two-storey box, which seems a less adventurous version of the Lord's media centre, on the other. It looks stylish, but stylish in a jumbled sort of way in which functions trump form. Behind the western stands a decent-looking block of flats has been built giving the whole an architectural presence and unity. Then comes the Trescothick stand, the Botham suites, the Colin Atkinson pavilion, the scoreboard, the Caddick pavilion (or 'Caddyshack') and the Ondaatje Stands, the totality like a parade of floats in a carnival, each one engaging and giving a garbled impression of unity. The whole is captivating in its way, but one thing that saves it from being ramshackle is the tall tower of St James's church holding sentinel at the south-west corner, assuming the mantle of Old Father Time at Lord's, a symbol of Taunton's longevity that intersects with the particularity of the game. England, now.

The church is a fine example of a Somerset tower, and while Somerset is famous for its cricket club, it should also be famous for its church towers. Pevsner's Buildings of England, so exact, so clinical, comes as near as Pevsner can to breaking into a eulogy. "Somerset Towers as a rule are square in plan . . . [They] are as a rule towers, in the sense that they have no spires . . . The big events were in square-topped towers. Quite a number of them are strikingly tall . . . But quite apart from height, an immense amount of thought was expended on the details . . . . There is hardly one amongst the fifty or so best towers which has not also its individual touches . . . [the individuality of the mason] is so fascinating to watch from place to place." Pevsner continues his analysis with such precision that in an age of hyperbole ('incredible', 'amazing', 'stunning') it feels like pedantry. And yet his measured words more truly measure the achievement.

In fact, two Somerset Towers are visible from the cricket ground, not just that of St James's, which is very close to the ground, but also that of St Mary Magdalene a quarter of a mile from the southern end of the ground, now hidden at certain points by the new Somerset Pavilion. Their visibility is increased by their height, St James's (below left) being 36.5m (120 feet) high, St Mary Magdalene's (below right) 50m (163 feet) high.

Their true majesty is best appreciated by standing close to them, but from the cricket ground their structure can be enjoyed too. Both towers

are subdivided horizontally into five stages: door level, stage one windows, stage two windows, stage three bell-chamber windows, finally battlements with pinnacles. At St Mary's this top is designed with pierced stone (see left) and the pinnacle edges rest on nothing, so both factors help the tower to soar even more.

Contributing to the creative visual effect is the verticality of their towers contrasted with the horizontality of the cricket ground. Those who breathed and moved in them over the decades are now gone, but you sense the generations that have gone before; for while the departed have gone, their souls are not necessarily departed. Do cricket grounds, like churches, house such souls? The administrators of Somerset Cricket Club certainly believe so, for round the ground panels are ranged that make up the Somerset Hall of Fame, the notable cricketers who have graced their county's game.

Is this like the aristocratic practice of placing portraits and busts of your ancestors round the house in order to encourage those coming after? The Romans had a concept of the *Di Penates*, Roman spirits connected with the inner part of the house. At the County Ground they seem to be everywhere, and one name in particular stands out, that of Harold Gimblett.

Intriguingly, at the foot of St James is tower is an area named Legend's Square.

We live in uncertain times: one of the markers of this condition is the floating apostrophe. Should it come before or after the 's'? Should it be there at all? Seeing the sign 'Welcome to Legend's Square' (above), I thought this was an error for 'Legends' [plural] Square', in honour of the assembled heroes who have trod the Elysian Fields of the county cricket ground. But further reflection made me realise that 'Legend's' [singular] is deliberate, since among those heroes one stands out, Harold Gimblett. There is supporting evidence in that the other name for this space is Gimblett Hill.

Fixed to the side of Gimblett Hill is the panel for this cricketing hero. The text begins: "The boy from Bicknoller became part of Somerset folklore when he scored a century in just 63 minutes on his début at Frome. He went on to become the county's leading first-class run-maker, scoring 49 centuries on the way." He played for the county from 1935 to 1954, so but for the war would no doubt have struck more still.

I had no more heard of Bicknoller than of Gimblett. It is a village north-west of Taunton lying at the foot of the Quantock Hills –

church, thatch, and hedge. Out of this secret place, where his family had farmed for many generations, came Harold Gimblett. The story of his county début, as the panel suggests, has something of the legendary about it. He was on a two-week trial for Somerset which looked to be ending unsuccessfully, but since they happened to be a player short for a match against Essex, Gimblett was summoned. The match was played at Frome, some sixty miles away along country roads, so he needed to get to Bridgwater where a lift awaited him. A bus would do it, but Gimblett missed it, so he hitched a lift in a lorry. In Somerset's first innings, they were 107 for 6, when he went in. Now came his chance, which he seized by turning his blade into a sword. His century came in 63 minutes and when he was out he had scored 123 runs. He helped take Somerset to 337, and they then bowled Essex out for 141 and 147, earning their victory by an innings. It was a fine example of the demoralising effect a whirlwind innings can have.

Had I dimly read about him in some cricketing history? I have no memory of doing so, but to come to Taunton was to meet his shade in person. It led to a subsequent acquaintance with David Foot's biography of the man published in 1984, six years after his death. The panel, very properly, records the successes of his life, but the biography reveals a tormented man who died from an overdose of sleeping pills. I was pulled up short by this contrast between success and failure, between facade and inner personality. There is a further dimension to his career, too. He did not live to see the explosive cricket that Twenty20 cricket has created, even in the Test arena, which on certain occasions achieves a kind of transcendental union between patient cricket and reckless cricket. A further reason for honouring him is that he discovered this before its time. Of all the heroes in the Somerset Hall of Fame, he must surely take pride of place.

So, get thee down to Taunton. For many people that is not a possibility because lives are too crowded, but for those lovers of cricket who are retired like myself, the pull in April to come and see a county match was irresistible. And so it was that in early August I found myself entering Taunton Cricket Ground feeling the pleasure of anticipation in just being present. I had no inkling what the next two months of county cricket would bring to my life.

2 ACT ONE: DUEL JEWEL

DAY ONE

The public story on the first day of the Somerset-Durham game was about Mark Wood picking up 3 wickets for 24 runs in 7 overs on his return to cricket after a spell of ankle surgery, having last played in a first-class contest in October 2015, in England's second Test against Pakistan.

Mark Wood bowling: Wood runs in with head well down, and in his bowling stride his right ankle twists markedly. His head and eyes face groundward just after he has released the ball.

With 3 wickets as well for Chris Rushworth, 2 for Graham Onions and 2 for Paul Coughlin, Somerset were seamed out for 184. [See scorecard at rear of book.]

The private story for me was about coming to Taunton's hallowed ground some distance from the big-city noise of places like The Oval and Edgbaston. I immediately warmed to the presence of the church of St James: as the day progressed the sun swung round it, moving it from being side-lit to back-lit. On a fine day I sat in the north-west stand in the afternoon with this silhouette against the blue sky and white cloud, while in the foreground figures in white cycled through their motions like the wheeling of the stars.

A further reassurance was provided by the sight of a tall but slightly portly figure marching to the wicket to open the batting for Somerset. Marcus Trescothick, no less, I gasped to myself, a name to conjure with for its exotic yet English quality, and from its link to past Ashes battles. In 2006 life went difficult for him; he departed from the limelight; and now, forty years of age, here he was returning, even if he had never in fact been away from Somerset. He biffed a 4, to my pleasure, but was out for 6, to my dismay. A fine knock before my eyes was not to be, nor was it in the second innings when he was out for a duck. It was a double disappointment, although for him perhaps it was 'another day, another cricket match, get on with it'. It would be quite wrong however to describe him as finished as he performed respectably in the batting averages for the season: 27 innings, 1,239 runs, at an average of 51.62. But that is not all. I remembered him as sharp in the slips for England. Here he was again, earning his place this time as much for his catching. He took two catches in each innings, all off the spinners. In the afterglow, I could not remember any dropped catches or half-chances put down. Old Faithful, he could be called: 33 catches for the season, thanks to a good pair of hands, and Somerset's predilection for spin bowling.

Trescothick signing autographs

There was another disappointment too. Paul Collingwood had also been a sterling performer for England between 2003 and 2011, also now forty years of age. He is as north-east England in background as Trescothick is south-west. He had 115 innings for England at an average of 40.36, but what I really recall was his fielding and catching which was of the fabled variety, the kind that made quarter chances into half chances, and half chances look easy. As I had reached the ground, I had looked forward to seeing him, but no reason was given for his absence, presumably an injury of some kind. Unkindly I thought it might be fatigue, or even, 'Must I go all the way to Taunton?' (I recalled a Norfolk anecdote, untrue I am sure but *bien trouvé*, that at the end of one season in the mythical past, football teams had combined to ensure it was Norwich City Football Club that got relegated and not some club from the centre of England on the grounds that the trip to Carrow Road in Norwich was too much off the beaten track.)

Collingwood's replacement was Gordon Muchall who had travelled down to Taunton in the morning. That intrigued me. Why had he not done so on the day before? What injury had Collingwood picked up that was not known about on the Wednesday? There will be a straightforward explanation for this, but it would take considerable detective work to find it out. Nor I suspect did it matter.

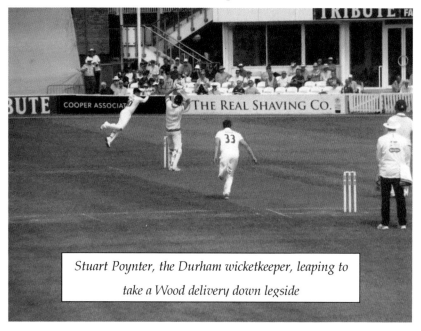

Stuart Poynter, the Durham wicketkeeper, leaping to take a Wood delivery down legside

Before I quite noticed it, Somerset were all out for 184, top scorer being Craig Overton, who is tall and aggressive with both bat and ball, out for 42. It was circa 2.45 p.m. when Durham started their innings, no doubt anticipating a juicy lead. It looked likely, as Mark Stoneman and Keaton Jennings jogged off some runs.

Jennings, standing in for Collingwood as captain, felt especially slow, but the run rate of 3 an over initially was reasonable, this being a 4-day game with a weather forecast without threat of stoppages. With 38 runs on the board, of which Stoneman had made 35, enter spin in the person of Jack Leach. In his first over he had Stoneman caught by Trescothick in the slips. It was quite unforeseen by me that spin was going to be king, having watched the Durham seamers at work. The Somerset crowd – if that is the right way to describe the spectators who, if bundled altogether, would have packed a stand or two, but who were dispersed in the wide range of sitting areas round the ground so that their loyalties and their applause were less contagious, more of a presence than a crowd – may have had shrewder ideas. They knew their team after all, even though Taunton has a reputation as a ground on which to score runs. Chris Rogers, the Somerset captain, knew best of all, for he brought Leach and Roelof van der Merwe on in the 11th and 12th overs respectively. My views were only conventional ones: the Durham seam quartet of Rushworth, Onions, Coughlin and Wood was a useful one, or, if understatement is too unfashionable, this was a powerful foursome of bowlers, and seeing it in action only prompted the spectator to imagine seam as the wicket-taker.

As it turned out, if seam was king, it was spin that was ace. For Somerset, Overton did well with pace and at the end of the day got the good wicket of Paul Coughlin when the score was 141. By this time

Twins: Roelof van der Merwe, left-arm spin, and Jack Leach, left-arm spin

Jack Leach (Jacko, Leachy) had taken 3 and his partner, van der Merwe (whom I christened VDM), 3.

I left the ground glowing from the late afternoon light and from having witnessed 30 overs of spin, a veritable feast. Among cricketological pleasures one is the sight of batsmen pinned down by spin, as Durham unexpectedly were. In short-form cricket the batsmen seek to hit their way out of trouble, often succeeding in doing so. For some reason it is harder in the long form of the game. Is it because the batsman is aware he has time? Be patient and master the spin? Let the spinner's fingers get tired? To an extent that is what happened here because it was Coughlin and Adam Hickey who put on 39 for the 7th wicket, until it was Overton's pace that did for Coughlin.

Apart from the effect of being bathed in light, why should I have glowed at the end of the day? It was the glow of contentment, which risked morphing into the glow of complacency. In a complicated world, heaving and shifting before our eyes, erupting into fearful public incidents and brutal news from the war zones, how could I be content? But I have always subscribed to 'the sacrament of the present moment', for there is a time to weep and a time to laugh, and a time to acknowledge pleasures experienced to the full. An even greater risk than complacency was musing nostalgically, "This is what England used to be like." Certainly, the presence of only four overseas players among the twenty-two on the field, and those four lending the proceedings an imperial touch (Rogers from Australia, Van der Merwe and Groenewald from South Africa, Poynter from Ireland), might have given a patriotic tinge to the glow, but in the words of that Norfolk heroine, Edith Cavell, patriotism is not enough. It is a merit of English cricket that it finds a place for overseas players, and a tribute to it that they wish to play here. In any case it works in reverse with English cricketers regularly spending time playing in Australia, India and elsewhere. Far from harking back to colonial days, I was wallowing in the full flush of globalised sport.

DAY TWO

I arrived in good time to queue for coffee without fretting that I would miss the first ball and consumed it pleasurably, since while the weather had more cloud than on Day One, it was warm and I sat once again in anticipation. You need to be ready. Viewed from the boundary, the players seem a bit mechanical, and then something happens that shows they are not. You have taken your seat not fully alert, but they have taken the field pepped up, and are looking for the decisive advantage. Overton bowls to Wood, Woody shoulders arms, the ball whistles past off stump, Ryan Davies behind the stumps gasps (visibly, not audibly) and Craigo puts hands on head in disbelief. Was the ball an inch or two away, or a foot away? Did Wood know exactly where his off stump was? These questions are beyond my conjecture, but in a way they have no bearing on the matter, for even in cricket with its built-in distanciation affects, theatrical performance is what we spectators have come to see. The moment is like an alarm going off. It is time to glue the eyes on the game. In this more awakened state, I chatted to a Somerset support, and listened to the accents around me. I heard Somerset burr naturally, but also Geordie accents. They had come a long way, I reflected, but combining first-class cricket (and a likely Durham victory) with a Somerset holiday, as I was planning myself, would be a sensible way to arrange a summer break.

On 141 on the day before, Wood had joined Hickey who was going well, and the score had moved close to Somerset's 184, both batsmen looking to be positive and succeeding. For the second over of the day Rogers brought on VDM, the more economical of runs on the first day, and after just two overs from Overton, he propelled Leach into the fray.

VDM bowling to Wood, beginning of Day Two

In his first over Wood hit Leach for 6 but seeking to repeat this trick on the next ball he was caught by Jim Allenby at first slip, for 27 good runs but out. A few minutes later, Chris Rushworth was lbw to VDM for a duck, and at 182 for 9 Durham were still three runs off a first-innings lead. This tiny passage of play began to generate its own suspense. Reason says it is not the case, but some seat of unreason in humans says that a small lead gives a psychological advantage. Naturally, a lead of 30+ runs in a low-scoring game gives an advantage which is more than psychological. Durham will have wanted that; Somerset will have felt that a decent second-innings score without having to spend time knocking off a deficit would license their spinners to rip through Durham a second time. The sight of Durham throwing away the advantage was dismaying for their supporters and compelling for Somerset ones – and for a neutral like myself who was so keen to see spin succeed.

Graham Onions is last man in and surely in his extensive career no stranger to making the opposition sweat for his wicket. He and Hickey take the scores level, and if Hickey can be supported in his run-making Durham can still get ahead; the timing of that final wicket is not pre-ordained. For Somerset, Leachy and VDM both have 4 wickets each: the contest is on between these two as to who can get the last. VDM has Onions to trap. For the last ball of his over, fine leg is brought in and a man put on the square-leg boundary. Who cares about a single being taken if Onions can be persuaded to slog the ball into his hands? If Onions does take a single this only brings him to face the first ball of the next over.

Onions is not persuaded either to slog or to seek the single, but off the first ball of Leach's next over, Hickey takes a single to leg thus bringing Onions on strike. Leach's first ball is too short and Onions drops the bat on it without trouble. The same with the next; and with the next. Leach must be doing this on purpose, I think, and so does Onions I'm sure. With the fifth ball of the over, the fuller ball beats the bat, although the sixth ball is nondescript.

So, VDM is on again. Hickey must have considerable confidence in his number 11 because he does not hesitate to take a single off the first ball. Onions has had no time to watch from close up. The second ball beats him; he gets his bat on the third; for the fourth Onions gets into his stride with a decent forward defensive; on the fifth he squeezes two runs past slip and prompts cries of 'Catch it'; the sixth Onions cuts along the ground to cover point but gets no run for this.

So, Leach's turn. Another single from Hickey, who must have concluded that either the situation is hopeless and therefore it is better to take runs wherever he can find them, or he has an admirable faith in Onions. The second ball goes past the bat; on the third Onions is lbw and Durham are 189 all out, a lead of 5 runs. Even though Durham have squeezed past them, the psychological advantage suddenly feels like Somerset's. Leach's figures are 19.3-2-69-5, while VDM's are 25-7-59-4. As they leave the field, Overton pats Leach on the back, and Leach puts his arm around the shoulder of VDM in muted triumph as they lead their team off.

96 overs were to be bowled in the day; we had had 16; so the 80 left offered a juicy prospect. Could Somerset push on and rattle off a

decent enough total to choke Durham into submission in the fourth innings; nor on reflection did they need to rattle them off, since there were still 2½ days to go. In view of the bowlers' dominance so far, the watchful accumulation of runs would do very well.

*

I have often felt that the pause between innings offers a moment of absorption, a relief from concentration. While the tension is lessened, the prospects for both teams can be weighed philosophically while the groundstaff perform their mysteries, the rituals providing a space for

thought. So I sat in meditation until I was jerked back to reality when the heavy roller was returned to its billet at the Somerset pavilion where I was sitting, this pregnant moment being disrupted by the roller squeaking as it rolled and prompting a spectator to shout, 'Have you run out of oil?'

It was time for the action to resume. When Middlesex played Yorkshire at Lord's in September 2015, a title-deciding match in fact, Ryan Sidebottom had Middlesex 0 for 3 at the end of the first over. I had gone to the game but had arrived twenty minutes after play had started so had missed this moment of high drama. But Providence kindly replayed a version of it at Taunton: at 11.54, Somerset were 0 for 3 in their second over. Trescothick, Abell and Rogers had all gone for a duck, two wickets to Rushworth, one to Onions, and for Tom Abell it was his second duck of the match. James Hildreth had to rescue things with Jim Allenby, but when Allenby was out, Somerset were only 33 runs for 6 wickets. It looked like the game would end on Day Two, I thought with consternation. I was anxious to see a full day's cricket, but mercifully salvation was at hand: 47 from VDM, the spin bowler; 49 from Davies, the wicketkeeper; and 38 from Overton, the fast bowler. When his 42 in the first innings is added in, Overton scored 80 runs in a match in which 689 runs in total were scored, so he got about 12% of that total. Pretty good for a fast bowler. You could tell that Craigo was really engaged in this contest.

Onions, Graham to me and Bunny to the Durham supporters, bowled well in both innings, with two wickets in the first and four in the second. I have always imagined him as youthful so it was disconcerting to see a touch of grey in his beard, an occupational feature of the truly seasoned pro.

Onions in action

Just before lunch an engaging cameo played out in front of me when a Durham supporter came to the fence bearing a cup of coffee and accosted Onions in the outfield. They were clearly old acquaintances because they struck up a conversation. With Durham ripping through Somerset, I heard the supporter comment, "I am booked in for four days of holiday," a complaint of a kind mixed with a good deal of *schadenfreude* at Somerset's discomfort.

Like the break between innings, lunch is also a time for reflection but in fact I was treated to a delightful interlude, as members of the Somerset visually-impaired team played on the outfield. After red-ball cricket there came white-ball cricket. Now, surely, big-ball cricket has a future also?

After lunch, VDM was bowled by Onions trying to hit a boundary in order to get to his 50. By this time Durham had got out their spinners too, but the leg breaks of Scott Borthwick (below), their number 3 bat, got clubbed.

Hickey on the other hand began to tie the Somerset big hitters down, clean bowling Overton. At 2.35 p.m. the number 11, Tim Groenewald, came to the crease, and helped Davies to hit a very valuable 52 runs for the last wicket before Davies was caught at slip off Hickey. On 49, and nervous like VDM at the prospect of getting a half-century, he had this enticing pleasure snatched away at the last moment.

So at 3.10 p.m., the match stood like this: Somerset 184 and 180, 364 in all, while Durham had 189, leaving them to get 176 for victory. To a non-participant such as myself this seemed perfectly manageable, for, while Somerset spin had undone Durham in the first innings, surely lessons had been learned. Watchfulness and positive batting would bring the target closer and closer to Durham's grasp, and by lunchtime on Day Three, the gap would have been closed, victory would be theirs, and Durham could begin its charge to win the County Championship. This was how they had talked coming into the match. After all, the pitch was only a day and a half old. From what the Somerset coach, Matthew Maynard, said at the end of the second day, I had the impression that he felt Durham seam had edged it: "It has been an absorbing game of cricket. Fair play to them [Durham], they have utilised the new ball brilliantly, especially in the second innings, when we knew that if we got off to a good start we could push on. But their seamers have got a lot more out of this wicket than we thought they would."

If Durham started their innings in hope, this did not stop Overton's fifth ball of his first over trapping Jennings lbw for 0, making his the 14th wicket of the day. Was Durham going to match Somerset in collapsing? It looked like it: they were 19 for 2 when Borthwick fell in the 7th over, but then, unlike Somerset, Durham started to repair their innings. Stoneman was playing very soundly and with Richardson he began to move Durham towards its target. However VDM in particular was making batting hard. Foot movement was the key to survival for the batsman, but the bowlers were kept constantly in hope. At the river end Leach was sticking to his task, but not taking wickets. Rogers, as he had been all through the Somerset bowling, remained creative, changing bowlers, changing ends. Overton came back and promptly beat the bat with good bounce. The next over Leach was brought back at the Somerset Pavilion end.

A stentorian voice rang out, "C'mon Somerset". The locals certainly could envisage a win. On the fourth ball of the over, the ball spooned above the head of first slip and was held. Why appeal softly when you can do so loudly? A resonant appeal followed, as night follows day, but was given not out. A Durham voice cried out, "You have to hit it first"; a Somerset voice replied, "West Country rules". I like this idea of being in a different land: it fitted in with the slogan on the Somerset shirt, 'Tribute – the South West's favourite ale.' This was news to me, but then Tribute is not drunk at all where I come from and I guess it is not swallowed in the north-east either. This was a refusal of globalisation, comfortable because it was of no consequence.

As Durham progressed I learnt something from conversation about Durham's financial woes which were leading to fears that all their players would get poached. Such talk in the club and in the press must have made it hard for the players to focus. If cricket is played in the mind, uncertainty about the future is debilitating. Winning the County Championship would help the club greatly and would motivate the players, but it was not going to wipe out the club's debt.

Following the drinks interval, VDM was brought back in place of Overton so he and Leach were again darting their missiles in tandem. In the 27th over, Davies missed a stumping off Leach, but with the next ball Leach had Richardson lbw. These excitements made for the tastiest kind of cricket. You anticipated wickets, but you also anticipated the batsmen fighting back with a boundary here or a rotation of the strike there. Richardson's wicket brought Muchall to the crease and I was told, with what reliability I was unclear, that he was going into teaching at the end of the season. He looked too young to stop playing first-class cricket, so I thought this was a sombre piece of information that seemed to mark a loss of confidence in his cricketing future, both for him personally and for the club. Still, he now had a chance to live for the moment, to play the hero. With his fourth ball of

the over, Muchall was beaten by bounce and missed it, but with the sixth ball he was off the mark.

At 102, Stoneman reached his 50, only a modest milestone until I reflected that it was the first 50 of the match. It had been a bowler's game, but a batsman scoring 100 or close to it could win the game for his side. Was this Stoneman's moment? His supporters were unsure: "Stoneman gets out on 50," I overheard a Durham supporter say in a downbeat way that seemed to come naturally. In the 31st over, VDM had a big appeal for lbw against Stoneman but it was not out: surely this was his moment to go well beyond 50? In the 34th, Muchall hit Leach for 4. Did this mean that Leach's fingers, perhaps his arm too, were getting tired? It must surely happen, if only Durham could wrestle him out of the game.

Yet VDM was bowling even more tightly than Leach and on the first ball of the 34th over, Stoneman reached forward to defend, the ball side-stepped the bat and span onto the stumps. A big moment, we all realised, and perhaps Stoneman too as he held the pose and pondered his position in the universe. Stoneman bowled van der Merwe 57; Durham 118 for 4; 58 runs for Durham to win, 6 wickets for Somerset to win. The ground had now entered its hour of perfection with the sun swinging lower to the west, and the grass beginning to glow. If I narrowed my eyes the players became silhouettes moving in patterns. In this vision, the details of play got lost but there was an overall sense that the game had gone a level nearer to paradise.

Stuart Poynter came to the wicket, a stocky man, and bearded too, another Edwardian grace note on this pre-war scene, World War One that is. There were 7 overs to go to the end of the day, and the instruction to him was surely to survive until stumps. 17 wickets had gone, enough for one day, but there was one more to come. At 5.50 p.m., Tresco's sound pair of hands snaffled Muchall at second slip off VDM. He was out for 17 valuable runs but I reckoned that this was 30 to 40 too few. A new nightwatchman was needed, so in came the Durham number 11, Bunny Onions. Despite all that had happened, my sense was that he was the man for the job: not just a competitor but an experienced competitor. When a Somerset voice shouted, "C'mon the boys," while I warmed emphatically to the sentiment my instinct was that Durham could still well win.

All that spin meant the 96 overs for the day soon came up. Durham ended it 130 for 5, needing 46 to win. Another day, another victory. We had had 31 overs of Somerset's spin, 16 from VDM (3 maidens, 2 for 40) and 15 from Leach (2 maidens, 1 for 45).

Onions striding to the pitch of the ball

That evening, I drove from Taunton to Porlock in a glow. I could not have asked for a better day's cricket. The road from Taunton, which I had never travelled before, needed all my attention, what with its switchback nature, and the sun descending into my direction of gaze. I swept past the turning for Bicknoller, suddenly a place to conjure with in my mind as Gimblett's village. There was an added factor to my state of intensity: I had not intended to go for a third day but surely I had to now? I would have to sleep on this to come up with an answer.

opposite page: end of Day Two

DAY THREE

Next morning, the answer was compellingly clear. Since the game had got to this delicate point, and even though I felt there would only be one hour of play (but what an hour!), I drove from Porlock to Taunton in good time to sit with a coffee in the sun and consult the auguries. Entry to the ground was free, exclamation mark. My journey felt worthwhile already.

It is not given to humans to predict the future with any certainty, but that does not stop them doing it. Naturally one regional newspaper, the Northern Echo, was inclined to favour Durham, but the other, the Western Daily Press, in a story buried well inside the paper, had "Somerset facing prospect of a stinging home defeat to Durham". And the anonymous Somerset fan on Grockles.com shared this pessimism, writing of the possibility of a defeat, only in this case it would be "valiant". Yet I thought the game finely balanced. I was particularly unimpressed by the phrase 'stinging defeat'. If Durham got the 46 needed for victory without further loss, then it would indeed be a stinging defeat. But then it should be bargained downwards: if Somerset took only one more wicket, then 'stinging' should be modified to 'severe', and two wickets would make it merely 'painful'. Three wickets taken would draw the sting pretty well, and four wickets would do so completely. If that was going to happen – Durham winning by one wicket – the excitement of the cricket would quite overshadow how to describe the defeat. From Durham's perspective, could Onions stick around to deter and demoralise

Somerset? His role would be to support Poynter as the key player to get Durham over the line. It was surely possible.

What was Chris Rogers going to do? He would surely have a 'never give up' attitude. So what bowlers would he use? Would Overton be asked – ordered, more like – to knock Onions over? The risk in that would be the leaking of runs before it happened. It would have to be VDM and Jack Leach doing the job with spin.

I moved from the coffee bar to take up position on the east side of the ground in order to be in the sun and watch the players emerge. Arriving at my seat, I got fascinated by the sight of VDM bowling at a single stump, first round the wicket, then over the wicket.

There was much huffing and puffing as he did so, but he hit the stumps several times. This was cricket's hard graft. For his part, Jacko was on the boundary doing some limbering up. Spin was definitely going to be Rogers' weapon of attack, and if it failed, the match would be lost.

It was not my job to rush over to North Street, to Castle Green, to High Street and urge everyone to come down to the cricket ground to watch an hour of high-intensity cricket, but in my imagination I thought of it. The ground was too sparsely populated for my liking, but I could console myself with the thought that every spectator was committed to one side or the other, and if there were any neutrals like myself even they were bewitched. As the players took the field, there were cries of "C'mon Somerset" and "C'mon Durham". I muttered a prayer: "O Lord, thou who hast brought us safely to the beginning of this day, and to this seat in this ground, grant that this contest be a good one." England, now.

Somerset take the field with a spring in their step

So Durham only needed 46 runs, Somerset only 5 wickets. There was all day to do it in. No need to hurry. Batsmen, bowlers, fielders, umpires, spectators, their job was to watch, wait, and play their parts.

Leach takes the ball; Onions is on strike. "C'mon Leachy" and "C'mon Jacko" ring out. On ball one, nothing happens, but his second

the end is nigh 1: Leach to Onions

ball produces an appeal for lbw which the umpire turns down. The third is more flighted and Onions digs it out. A small victory for him, but then the fourth ball goes past the bat. The fifth ball hits the pad, Somerset appeal, and the finger ascends. Like countless lbw victims before him, Onions stands rueful: how did that happen? Surely I was not lbw? How could I be Leg Before Wicket? Only a Shakespearean soliloquy could do justice to what he is thinking.

The new bat is Paul Coughlin. Although he made 30 in the first innings, in a low-scoring match, the task of doing so again feels daunting. But if he does, he propels Durham to victory surely? Durham supporters encourage him from the sidelines. Yet these thoughts are will-of-the-wisps. On his first ball he is caught out mentally, and caught literally. I am taken unawares too, because I had intended to get my camera on this ball but in the tension I'd been slow to do so and, as I was learning, spinners don't give you time. The bald words will have to do for the image: Coughlin caught Allenby bowled Leach 0. Durham still need 46 runs, but now have only 3 wickets left.

The 'stinging defeat' is being consigned to the Somerset dustbin and the contents plonked in the Durham dressing room.

The new bat is Adam Hickey who made 36 in the first innings, while Poynter, who had looked solid at the close of Day Two, but who has yet to face a ball this morning, is at the other end. VDM now has the ball but despite his bowling practice he is the one with the nerves. His first two balls Poynter cuts to cover point, and the third is again too short but this time Poynter cuts it to the boundary. The fourth ball is a pleasant single to deep midwicket. Hickey is the new batsman; he is a left-hander so VDM has to adjust his line, and his fifth and sixth balls are blocked.

43rd over: 3 wickets needed for Somerset, 41 runs for Durham. Leach bowls to Poynter, surely the key batsmen to remove? The first ball he plays with a forward defensive. Good feet. For the second ball on the other hand his feet are not so good: Leach appeals for lbw and is granted his request. Poynter is out for 12, and Durham are 135 for 8.

The new bat is Mark Wood, a bowler of course but he can hit the ball as witnessed by his 27 in the first innings. On the other hand, his injury has meant that he has not been much at the batting crease this season. He is not perhaps the person to base a tail-end fightback on. Somerset play mind games. Leach's third ball, Wood's first, produces cries of dismay as a wicket does not materialise. The second ball has the same effect, except the cries are less *forte* than for the previous ball. For the fifth ball, the cries of 'Oh!' are more ritualised. Wood is winning, and for the sixth ball, the ball spins from his bat so that slip has to run for it. Wood gets off the mark, and he will face

VDM whose first over was less convincing than Leach's. Can he dig in?

40 runs needed: so near and yet so far. 2 wickets needed: so near and yet so far. On his first ball from VDM, Wood looks solid. But the gods are not in his favour, nor is the pitch; the bowler certainly isn't. The second ball, bouncing unexpectedly, pops off the shoulder of the bat to Tresco at second slip. Somerset can surge to victory. Chris Rushworth, Durham's sterling fast bowler, is the number 11. He survives his first ball from VDM but on the second, he is caught by Allenby.

the end is nigh 2: Allenby about to catch Rushworth in the slips

the end has come: Durham are 136 all out, and Somerset win by 40 runs.

Van der Merwe has figures of 17.4 overs, 45 runs, 4 wickets. Leach has 17 overs, 46 runs, 4 wickets. No wonder they lead Somerset off the pitch shoulder to shoulder: they are identical twins.

I came, I saw, they conquered – in 22 balls. Game over, except that it was not over since from this point on the mind recollects both the facts of the game and one's perceptions of the game, merging them all in one radiant memory. Like raw meat, it needs a quick sear to seal in the juices, then a slow braise to bring out the flavours.

I could not bring myself to depart immediately but hung around with my camera in case of some further off-field excitement or interest. As I stood near the Caddyshack, voices rose in harmony in a song of victory. Not the Durham lot, but the Somerset team in full voice singing their anthem, a Wurzels song called 'The Blackbird'. The first stanza goes like this:

All me life I'm on the farm, workin' for me keep

tending pigs and chickens, and they cows and sheep

but everywhere I'm working, there's one who always mocks me

he hidin' somewhere in the trees, blackbird I'll have he.

And the chorus goes like this:

Where be that Blackbird to? I know where he be,

he be up yon Wurzel tree, and I be after he!

Now I sees he, and he sees I,

buggered if I then get 'en

with a girt big stick I'll knock him down

Blackbird I'll 'ave he!

Suffice it to say that this ballad stretches over four stanzas and climaxes with the life-affirming, even if wildlife-denying, lines:

If I chase him long enough, I'll get 'en bye and bye,

and celebrate my vict'ry with a girt big blackbird pie!

This photo of the Caddyshack is nondescript but it has to be imagined with a soundtrack, what the academic theorists might label an 'absent presence', namely the sound of the Somerset players in full voice. Although I am from Norfolk, I am not rustic, but I have been familiar with jocund rusticity in this part of the world. Cricket crowds are in the big city, cricket money comes from global television rights, cricket headlines are not aimed at readers of the Western Daily Press or Eastern Daily Press. Yet here was cricket's pumping heart: a green lawn, trees and hills in the distance, a church glowing in the sun, and the run-stealers, the ball-spinners, the catch-snaggers at play. I hoped that Chris Rogers, born in Sydney, Australia, way out back of Wurzel Land, was leading the chorus.

I continued to hang around in the sun. The stands were empty, but there were still people about in groups. I could see one or two Durham players with their kit heading off, with the long drive home and a fourth day suddenly freed up. They would have preferred to be still playing cricket, I felt sure. The Somerset players, on the other hand, could use the full day to savour the win. Their next county match was on 23rd August, 16 days away. Could they propel themselves into contention for the Championship trophy?

As I strolled about, suddenly I saw Jack Leach on the bench talking to someone – a friend, an elder statesman of the club, a sponsor. I had no idea. I decided to take a photo of him as I could not resist.

When he looked up, I felt I owed him something for letting me take his photo, so I congratulated him on his bowling, and then volunteered something like, "The headline in the local newspaper said that Somerset faced a stinging defeat. I'm from Norwich, but I felt that was not right." That prompted his interlocutor to offer to take a photo of me with Leach, which he did. Not a selfie but, I have to admit, an image in the same spirit. These things happen by grace, and this image pins the whole three days in my mind.

Back in Porlock, I came across the pavilion for Porlock Cricket Club, which, as I learned from peering through the windows, was founded in 1865 and had its own Hall of Fame in the form of a board of photographs of players, all beginning to fade. The pavilion, it must be admitted, is very forlorn. Yet if it is unloved in general, it is loved by me because it is a metaphor for long-form cricket: it is a survivor.

Each season county cricket produces some jewels. Middlesex versus Yorkshire in 2015 was one of them. Was Somerset versus Durham in 2016 another? Perhaps not: four low-scoring innings of 184, 189, 180 and 136. If you read that, you would rightly conclude it was a bowler's game. But in a bowler's game, Mark Stoneman's 57 in Durham's second innings moves from good to outstanding. 20 runs more from him and I felt sure Durham would have won the game.

42 overs then 59 overs in the two first innings, 41 overs and 45 in the second two. But here it becomes topsy-turvy. All but two of the Somerset wickets fell to seam bowling; all but three of the Durham ones to spin. Of the total number of balls bowled by Somerset, 637, van der Merwe and Leach bowled 475 of them, almost exactly three quarters. It was worth travelling a long way just to watch all that spin. Every ball seemed to have interest, and it makes for a quick version of long-form cricket as the overs rattle along.

There was another, larger dimension to Somerset's victory. On 20th July, after some 10 matches played in Division One of the County Championship, Durham was on 128 points, 13 behind the leaders Middlesex and with a game in hand. Somerset by contrast were fifth on 119 points, and with fears of relegation by no means completely banished. On 7th August after this crunching victory they were second in the table on 138 points to Middlesex's 146. Down the necks of both teams breathed the dragon of Yorkshire with 137 points – and a game in hand. But Somerset had its tail up.

Durham by contrast faced a difficult month. Their hopes of winning the championship were gone, and they risked, albeit remotely, the jail of relegation. They lost to Middlesex in their next game, drew with Warwickshire and Nottinghamshire, and then lost to Yorkshire. They were now sixth in the table with 154 points, and two games to go. It was time to rally, which they did to beat Surrey and Hampshire, thus ensuring no relegation. Yet it was to no avail: their financial troubles had led to an ECB bail-out, the price of which was enforced relegation to Division Two, with the additional insult of a 48-points handicap being imposed. Truly, defeat could be stinging.

3 ENTR'ACTE: WIDENING AND DEEPENING

On 7th August, in the wider County Championship, Yorkshire I felt were in charge. This may have shown disrespect to Middlesex who were leading the table, but a neutral would argue that Yorkshire, still with a strong team despite their very best being on England duty, winners of the Championship in the previous two seasons, captained by the pugnacious Andy Gale and coached by a motivating Australian, Jason Gillespie, was the team to back.

For some curious reason I was no longer neutral, at least for a month or two. Somerset had shown their credentials in seeing off Durham, and were clearly motivated to go for the finishing line with an admirable tenacity. What was more, they had a more profound reason than any other team to take the County Championship: they had never won it in their history. Leicester City had stirred the hearts of all lovers of the underdog with their winning of the Premier League earlier in the year. They were setting Somerset the perfect example.

In the next round, on 23rd to 26th August, Somerset drew with Hampshire but garnered 13 points in doing so. Yorkshire showed their mettle by beating Nottinghamshire to win 21 points. Middlesex had beaten Durham earlier in the month to win 22 points. The table now read:

Middlesex   173 points from 12 games

Yorkshire   168 points from 12 games

Somerset   151 points from 12 games.

In the next round after that, 31st August to 3rd September, rain either spoiled things or set them up nicely, according to your point of view. Somerset, Yorkshire and Middlesex all drew, the first two taking 10 points to Middlesex's 9. For the next round, 6th to 9th September, the logjam needed to shift; pedigree would need to be on display. All three showed it by winning their games, Middlesex beating Nottinghamshire, Yorkshire beating Durham and Somerset beating Warwickshire, even if by only 31 runs. 19-year-old Dominic Bess, with his right-arm off breaks, made his Championship début and took 6 for 28 in the first innings, while Leach took 6 for 42 in the second. The table then looked like this:

Middlesex   202 points

Yorkshire   201 points

Somerset   180 points.

Two rounds remained. In the penultimate round, on the 12th to 15th September, Lancashire were to play Middlesex in Manchester, Yorkshire to play Somerset in Leeds. All parties prayed that rain was not going to spoil the party which was likely to consist of Yorkshire trouncing Somerset, and Middlesex battling Lancashire to a tight win or a draw, leaving the two big clubs to contest the County Championship in a super final at Lord's on 20th September.

But the future is elusive. The above script was certainly not observed, and we were informed it would not be by the end of the first day when Yorkshire were bowled out for 145 and Somerset ended the day on 107 for 1. All the Somerset bowlers chipped in, with three wickets for Overton and for Allenby, two for Groenewald, one each for Gregory and Trego. Leach however was wicketless, something he would remedy in the second innings. As I was a Leach fan by now, I had to console myself with the thought that the pitch was not right for him. Yet I felt sorry for Yorkshire: perhaps being a game behind the others was catching up with them, but I pulled myself together – this soft attitude was unlikely to be shared by Gillespie or Gale.

Day Two was no better for them. Somerset were all out for 390, 245 ahead, and Yorkshire ended the day 57 for 3, still 188 runs behind. A massive fightback would be needed to get sufficient runs on the board to allow even their formidable quintet of bowlers – Sidebottom, Brooks, Plunkett, Bresnan and Rashid – to snuff out Somerset, no longer a guttering flame more a roaring fire. Nor was it to be, for despite 116 from Jake Lehmann and 73 from Liam Plunkett, Yorkshire were all out for 286 thanks to Jack Leach again coming into his own with figures of 6 for 64 in 24.3 overs. Somerset only needed 41 to win, Trescothick and Abell duly obliging without loss.

Yorkshire eyes could only turn to Lancashire. If they could defeat Middlesex, and Yorkshire beat the latter at Lord's, the title could still be theirs, provided Somerset knew their place and did not defeat Nottinghamshire so thoroughly at Taunton as to make up the one-point deficit they held on Yorkshire. On the other hand, if Middlesex defeated Lancashire, then the title was theirs firmly to lose at Lord's.

At 258 for 3, Middlesex were going well at the end of Day One. On Day Two, they were all out for 327 and Lancashire ended on 102 for 5. East of the Pennines Yorkshire will have been anxious. However the Lancashire newcomer Rob Jones was 42 not out, and on Day Three not only went on to his century but was not out when all the other 10 wickets had fallen. Lancashire ended 68 runs behind, but Middlesex were beginning to run out of time when at the end of the day they were 72 for 4 scoring at a rate of 2 an over. Optimists in Yorkshire will have predicted a draw, even if pessimists feared Middlesex pulling off a dramatic victory.

The optimists were right, and when their predictions came true, the rest of us could rejoice for on 15th September going into the final round the table stood thus:

Middlesex   213 points

Yorkshire   204 points

Somerset   203 points.

It meant that all 3 teams were in the chase for the line. Middlesex and Yorkshire were neck and neck, but even if Yorkshire were to beat Middlesex, a Somerset victory of sufficient magnitude could take them to a photo finish.

4   ACT TWO: LONG-FORM RULES OK

The final round was scheduled for 20th to 23rd September, Tuesday to Friday. The summer had been a good one, so good that I went swimming several times in the North Sea. There was a strange atmosphere in the country in general. In the referendum on 23rd June, the majority had voted to Leave the European Union, but then nothing seemed to happen (barring the small matter of a change of Prime Minister), as if the continuing good weather was continuing to hold us in its thrall. I thought of the French words for phoney war in 1939 – 'drôle de guerre', i.e. 'a funny sort of war'. War had been declared but nothing much seemed to happen. The vote on 23rd June felt important at the time and as it receded into the past only more so. Much of what journalists write is barely the first draft of history, and a lot of it does not make the second draft. When historians get down to the third draft, the June referendum will still be there.

The climax of the 2016 County Championship will not make it into a political or economic history of the UK, although it might just merit a footnote in a cultural one. World cricket is surrounded by a debate both intriguing and forceful about the relative merits of short-form and long-form cricket. The former draws the money and produces rushes of excitement, but lacks the absorbing quality of the long game that purists would argue is its essence, what makes it different from all other games, where paradoxically, mystically perhaps, a boring passage of play can enhance the whole. The long-form game has that quality, but is not successful in the modern sense where things are valued by numbers, targets and financial returns. The County Championship has been the backbone of English cricket since it came about in the 19th century. We had a clear understanding of our role in the world then, but what should that be now? The referendum showed how uncertain we have become. Would the County Championship end with a whimper? Would it only reinforce doubts about the future? Would it provide ammunition to the optimists or the pessimists? Would it be hard? Would it be soft?

In 2015 I had been reminded how great a game the four-day version of cricket could be when I had attended the climax of the season at Lord's, when Middlesex played Yorkshire. It went to four days; it began with Ryan Sidebottom bowling a triple-wicket maiden over, yet from 0 for 3 Middlesex went on to win the match. Despite this, Yorkshire won their second consecutive County Championship. I had been so entranced by the match that I turned the photographs of it with accompanying text into a book, 'Cricket's Pure Pleasure'.

It enjoyed modest but welcome sales over the 2016 season. The schedule showed Middlesex and Yorkshire meeting again in September, and it seemed the obvious thing to experience cricket's pure pleasure again. I set my face against it early on. It may be a cliché but it is surely true: lightning does not strike twice in the same place. Or as the Greek philosopher Heraclitus said more originally (and his words have not suffered the repetition that turns them into a cliché), 'No man ever steps in the same river twice, for it's not the same river and he's not the same man.' Even though by midsummer it looked as if the game would be a crucial one, who could guarantee this? What if the weather ruined it? What if it all proved to be an unexploded firework?

My wife Maggie had not accompanied me to Taunton, and even as I enthused in the following weeks about the twists and turns in the County Championship, we had laid plans to go to Italy towards the end of September, with flights and accommodation all booked. Cricket may have beckoned, but so did the prospect of some intensive sightseeing in that seductive country in beautiful early-autumn weather. That was the plan to prevail, with the consequence that we were due to fly to Bologna on Day Three (the Thursday) of the final round of matches, while Days One and Two were spent getting ready. In making that decision, I felt I was participating in an allegory about the referendum: where did my loyalties lie? With the CIPP, the Cricket Is Paramount Party, or with Europe?

As it turned out, my loyalties could be towards both. In Norwich on Days One and Two, I followed the games in the final round online, reading about them if not ball by ball, then some of the time over by over, and certainly session by session. Its needle quality was such that it attracted the moneyed classes at Sky Sports who opted to screen the game at Lord's. I do not have ready access to this, so my main option was to listen to commentary on BBC radio, and marvellous it was: the voices, drawn I understood from local radio, were new to me, the sentiments gently expressed, the partisanship manifested in subtle and courteous ways. What they really wanted to convey was that long-form cricket be appreciated for the marvel that it is. And the circumstances created a paradox in that tiny events became massive. To be present at the game is the closest encounter of all, and to see it on television and hear it on radio, in real time, is to experience it at only one remove. Following online is a third-remove experience. And there is now a fourth remove, like a fourth dimension: the chaff on Twitter. From all these modes of encounter, you could feel that the only places to be on the planet were either at Taunton when Bess, with Somerset 9 wickets down, took their first innings past 350 to give them a fourth batting point, or at Lord's when Sidebottom took Yorkshire past 350 (Yorkshire having been 53 for 4 on Day Two). These tiny little resurrections stirred a cheer among the relevant supporters, and the thrill of emotion amongst the rest of us.

I enjoyed close contact with the two matches on the first two days, but what would happen on Day Three when we would be cocooned in an aeroplane and out of contact with the real world?

DAY ONE

The story started in Taunton. Somerset won the toss, a small kindness to them from the cricket-loving gods (of which there must be a number, you feel), and proceeded to pull the Nottinghamshire bowling apart – up to a point. For the third wicket, Rogers and Hildreth put on 269 runs, Rogers making 132 in what would turn out to be his last match for Somerset, so that was the stuff of fable. Equally so was Hildreth's 135, for early on he had been struck on the ankle by Jake Ball's ball and was reduced to only one fully functioning leg. He hobbled, while young Abell ran for him – for four hours. Then Ball struck again, and repeated it to such effect that Somerset went from 322 for 5 to 322 for 9. A thought should be spared for Nottinghamshire. Since they were already relegated, they had the challenge of motivating themselves for this match, a challenge it turned out that was beyond them as a team. However Jake Ball, ambitious still to play for England, got 6 wickets for 57 runs at a rate of 2.19 per over. Cricket is a team game enriched by striking individual performances. As the day wore on, thanks to Rogers and Hildreth, Somerset were looking for a score of 400 and five gold-dust batting points. At 322 for 9, thanks to Ball, a fourth batting point looked beyond them, let alone a fifth.

At Lord's, the play seemed less cavalier, but no less compelling, the only sour note being the weather, causing an hour to be lost to bad light at the end of the day. Should we conclude then that the gods are indifferent to cricket? Perhaps, but they could have been so much more vindictive by washing out a whole day's play. Only 208 runs were scored in the day off 82 overs, and at one point Middlesex were 97 for 4. That they were rescued from a position that threatened defeat, and no trophy, was due to Nick Gubbins who was 120 not out at the end of the day, while his captain, James Franklin, was on 21. Unlike 2015, Sidebottom was not in the wickets, but Yorkshire have a terrific bowling attack which is marked by its variety. When one misses another hits. Here it was Jack Brooks taking three big wickets in the day.

DAY TWO

As I have indicated, long-form cricket makes big dramas out of micro-moments. At Taunton, Leach and Bess walked out to resume the Somerset innings, needing 28 runs to reach 350. But these two are spin bowlers not batsmen! Yet by defensive craft in Leach's case and by mixing boundaries with nurdles in Bess's case they made it, and

Somerset were eventually all out for 365, Leach 2 not out, Bess caught Lumb bowled Patel 41.

No doubt buoyed by this exploit, Leach and Bess then became the dismantlers of Nottinghamshire's first innings. The highest scorer was Jake Libby on 42, and inner demons, aided by the spinning ball, condemned them to 138 all out. Bess had figures of 5 for 43, Leach 3 for 42. By the end of the day, Somerset were 105 for 2 and since they were now 332 ahead of Nottinghamshire they were stretching well out of sight. Somerset was telling the teams at Lord's that they were right on their tail, and that they were minded to snatch the trophy.

At Lord's, thoughts were on the matter in hand. The day began as Yorkshire's as they got Middlesex all out for 270, Brooks ending on 6 for 65. It then became Middlesex's thanks to Toby Roland-Jones who took 4 wickets. At one point Yorkshire were 53 for 4, and would have been 87 for 5 if a hard-handed Compton had not put Hodd down in the slips. It was a psychological turning-point as Tim Bresnan, formerly of England and a cricketer of sterling qualities who had risen up the order in 2016 by virtue of his improved batting, went on to end the day unconquered on 72. Yet they still needed 115 more to get the 4 batting points that would match Somerset's and thus keep them one point ahead. The 41 overs in which they had to achieve this (since batting points can only be earned from the first 110 overs of an innings) were less of a problem than the fact that they had only four wickets left.

I had not bothered with Twitter on Day One, but on Day Two I began to. The commitment of the supporters on the different sides was admirable. But were neutrals commenting as well? Then it occurred to me that neutrality was difficult to achieve, perhaps impossible. Living in Norfolk, I was a prime candidate to be neutral, but that godlike position had been severely compromised. When I learned that Somerset had never won the championship, that Tresco at the end of his career was as deserving a candidate as anyone, and after I had seen them in masterful action in August, not least the Specsavers icon, the spectacle-wearing Jack Leach, I was clear that I wanted them to go all the way. This meant the other two prize-fighters would have to wrestle themselves to an exhausting draw. But if that wasn't going to happen, which did I want to win? Middlesex play at Lord's so they should win? Irrational, but it did occur to me. I had seen their famous victory in 2015, so it would be right for them to win again and this time take the trophy. Yorkshire victory on the other hand would be the result of a bulldog spirit allied to technical brilliance, the ingredients of great cricketing teams. I could only gasp in admiration at Bresnan's performance. Only one thing counted against them: they were top dogs, and as I fondly imagined, CIPP members favoured the underdog.

DAY THREE

Italy beckoned. On reaching Ferrara, I was only able to log into my tablet at 2.38 p.m. to discover that Yorkshire were on 349 for 9, needing only one run to get to 350 with 4 overs in hand. But rain had held up play.

In Taunton by contrast the sun shone on Somerset who had declared on 313 for 5, Rogers having made his second century in the match. Nottinghamshire had the small matter of batting a day and a half to make 541 runs in order to win. At 2.38 p.m. they were 54 for 2, still with a long way to go. Maggie and I rested for an hour, and I logged on to check progress, then we sallied forth to the Castello Estense (below) in the centre of Ferrara, the solid fortress begun in 1385 from which the D'Este family conducted their own Renaissance.

As an edifice, it verges on the colossal, and is surrounded by a considerable defensive moat. In the centre of this city of severe lines that are echoed in the paintings of Giorgio De Chirico, who was invalided there in 1915 to 1918, and in the films of Michelangelo Antonioni, born and brought up in Ferrara, there were no trees visible – nor any sign of interest in the cricketing contest 700 miles away. It would have felt austere and as far from the greensward of an English cricket ground as could be, were not the severity of the city softened by the late afternoon sunlight so that the streets and buildings seemed to glow. Instead of figures in white against green there were bicyclists everywhere, their backlit silhouettes wheeling past and away in their own patterning.

Ferrara centre in evening light

When I got back to our flat at the end of the day, Somerset had beaten Nottinghamshire who were 215 all out within the day, in which only

Billy Root, the brother of Joe, quixotically struggling to do all he could for his home county of Yorkshire, troubled the scorers at all significantly with a 66 not out. The spin trio of Bess, Leach and van der Merwe had bowled 49 of the 63 overs in the innings and done the damage: Bess's figures were 0 for 34, Leach 4 for 69, and VDM 3 for 59.

Over in the big city of London, Middlesex and Yorkshire carried on their prize-fighting. Yorkshire had swept past the 350 mark and were all out for 390. Middlesex were 120 runs behind on their first innings and had got to 81 for 2 by the end of the day. Gubbins and Malan were going well, Gubbins for the second time in the match. If Middlesex were going to win, a lot would be due to him. However, I felt that Somerset were now favourites: they had played powerfully in the manner of champions apart from a bad wobble on 322 in the first innings, to garner 23 points. The table now read:

Somerset   226 points

Middlesex   218 points

Yorkshire   211 points

If Middlesex won their match they would have 234 points. If Yorkshire won they would add 16 points for the grand total of 227, one point ahead of Somerset. The drama surrounding the extra batting point for each side was not a superficial one.

There was motivation enough for both teams, but it still remained difficult to imagine a result at Lord's other than a draw. Bresnan was reported in The Times as saying the final hour of play was like fighters eyeing up each other before trading punches again. Was the final day to produce some brutal knockout?

And here I was in a foreign country. Maggie reminded me that there was a subplot in Alfred Hitchcock's *The Lady Vanishes* relevant to our situation. Made in 1938, the story revolves wittily and suspensefully round the sinister complexities of Mittel Europa politics, peace fraying in presage of the most murderous war. Hitchcock was responsible for the thrills, the script writers, Sidney Gilliat and Frank Launder, for the wit. They created a comic subplot about two caricature Englishmen abroad, Charters and Caldicott, trying to get back to England so as not to miss the Test Match, only to be impeded from this blinkered pursuit by snow and international intrigue. Played by Basil Radford and Naunton Wayne, although I could not tell you which played which, nor whether Charters and Caldicott had Christian names, they were comic types, the script satirising their obsession with cricket and their indifference to everything going on around them. Indeed they were proto-members of the Cricket Is Paramount Party that may have played a role in the referendum debate. Eurosceptics, no doubt. Isolationists? In their way, but then what were they doing holidaying in Mittel Europa – or in Caldicott's

words, "a third-rate country" – at the beginning of the film?

Their frequent appearances weave in and out of the film, usually exasperated because they want information on what is

happening in the Test Match. When the heroine suggests that the cricket is of no importance, Charters comments, "If that's your attitude, there's no more to be said." At the end, they arrive in London only to find that rain has washed the match out.

Seventy years later, such ignorance is impossible. Equipped with all the necessary gadgetry, I could have followed the match online ball by ball. I could have listened to radio commentary ball by ball. No doubt, I could have watched it on a supercharged, ethereally connected tablet on the plane, at Bologna airport, in Ferrara itself. (My tablet in fact is like an old banger that gets me from A to B but not in any supercharged way.) Anyway, I had gone to Ferrara to sightsee. A climax in the County Championship such as I was witnessing only comes along very rarely, but when there is so much to see in the world, I needed to take in Ferrara for fear of not doing justice to that mesmerizing place. I was at risk of muddling my categories: following the cricket when I should be sightseeing; sightseeing when I should be following the cricket. I suppressed the risk by concentrating on Ferrara, but I was not completely lost to the cricket.

opposite page: Ferrara skyline at 9 pm, end of Day Three

DAY FOUR

Somerset could only watch, which is what masochistically they chose to do. The team, the members and the supporters all gathered in the ground to do so: the team sat in the 1875 Club, the members in the Colin Atkinson Pavilion and the supporters in the Stragglers' Cafe. It must have been an agonising bonding exercise.

In Ferrara that morning, we devoted the time to cycling around the walls that hem in the Renaissance city.

These are Herculean for two reasons, because they were built by Ercole I d'Este (1431-1505) and because they are massive (so much so that their construction seriously weakened the city financially). But they have not fallen and they define Ferrara as much as the Castello, the Duomo, the Palazzo dei Diamanti and other buildings. It is to these walls that the trees have migrated, so that cycling beneath them, then cycling along the top of the walls, and making a complete circuit, proved profoundly satisfying.

I did not engage with the cricket until 1 o'clock. Middlesex were now 239 for 3, 117 runs ahead, thanks to Gubbins and Malan, so the game seemed headed for a momentous draw. But from afar I watched the game enter a bizarre period of turbulence. At 1.15 p.m. here was Adam Lyth coming on to bowl for Yorkshire, and Alex Lees soon after. Something odd had happened. Not being glued to the game, I had not realised that Gale had left the field three times to negotiate a declaration with James Franklin, the Middlesex captain. Their conversations would make a good piece of theatre, especially as Franklin revealed later that he was on the toilet at the time they took place. The target of 210 off 30 overs (7 an over) was put on the table (presumably by Middlesex) and declined; then 210 off 32 overs (6.9 an over). At 240 off 40 overs (6 an over) a deal was done. A farcical period ensued with the batsmen clubbing deliberately soft bowling. How contrived this was may be gauged by the comment on the BBC online commentary when Lees bowled Simpson for 31: "I have never seen someone more disappointed to take a wicket."

Regular watchers of county cricket know about declarations being made to manufacture a result in the interest of entertainment for both spectators and players. Was this occasion different? The match was a Championship decider; one of the parties was excluded from the negotiations; while it was not true that the nation was watching, there was a huge turnout from the CIPP. The essence of it is this: the heart does not like it, but the head can see the point of it, that the result is not being fixed, the match is merely being reset in order to produce a win or lose result, about which there was no certainty at this stage.

Something is happening in cricket to the idea of the drawn game. In my youth, they seemed to be a regular occurrence, but developments have reduced their number. First there has been the very welcome one of trying to outwit the weather and to ensure that as many overs as possible are bowled. Secondly, fast-form cricket seems to be playing an intangible part. In 1997, half of all Tests ended in a draw (21 draws in 44 games); in 2016, there were 47 Tests but only 7 draws. Yet a hard-fought draw can give exquisite pleasure to the spectator watching in real time, even if the bald match report, 'match drawn', trashes that pleasure. Certainly victory for one side or the other is now felt to trump a drawn result. After all, it is the spirit of the age: who dares, wins. We do not say: who dares, draws.

So, in manufacturing a climax at Lord's, heads and hearts came into it, in order to set the pulse racing. Down in Taunton, blood began to boil. A drawn game was not a boring end, for Somerset would be champions, and in a thrilling manner. Instead a result was being pursued that would deny them their glory. Yet in the aftermath the angels prevailed: Matthew Maynard, the Somerset coach, admitted that they would have done the same as Middlesex and Yorkshire. Franklin and Gale were both generous in their comments, Gale in particular: "I told James Franklin that we would go for it and I'm a man of my word." On Saturday 24th September, The Times ran an intriguing piece under the headline 'Was declaration bowling a fair tactic?' Doug Grattan argued no, cogently. Josh Burrows argued yes, cogently. It was Burrows however who came up with the killer simile, and here the angelic host showed a demonic streak: ". . . With the title at stake, expecting Middlesex and Yorkshire to extend [Somerset] the same sympathy is like expecting two pitbulls not to fight for the sake of the cat that lives next door." In prize-fighting parlance, the two heavyweights were not going to stand aside for the contestant perceived as a middleweight.

Immediate opinion was that the title had been handed to Yorkshire, since 240 off 40 overs was likely to be completed in a canter. This target turned out in fact to have been contrived with great finesse, a tribute to Franklin's and Gale's cricketing brains. To quote George Dobell on Cricinfo, the target was "tantalising enough to seduce Yorkshire but distant enough to defend". As in all successful negotiations, both sides felt a win was in their grasp – at least at 2.40 p.m. when Yorkshire came out to bat.

About that time I had forsaken the quick to visit the dead. In any Ferrara Hall of Fame, beside multiple members of the D'Este family, would be the film-maker Michelangelo Antonioni (1912-2007) and the novelist Giorgio Bassani (1916-2000). Antonioni is buried in the Certosa Cemetery in the north east corner of Ferrara, a mass assembly of graves, perfectly ordered and dominated by the imposing presence of the Certosa church.

How was I to find this particular tomb, I wondered, but I was helped to do so by the cemetery office. In block M12, there is a 'street' of tomb houses, one of which belongs to the Antonioni family. Peering in I saw Michelangelo's name, and felt a sudden encounter with his shade, such as

I had experienced at Taunton learning about Harold Gimblett. The dead communicate to us, in Eliot's phrase, "beyond the language of the living".

If this was true of the Certosa Cemetery, it was doubly so of the Jewish cemetery in the same north-east quarter of the city.

Its forebidding gates stand locked at the end of the Via Vigne, but ringing a bell we were let in by a caretaker who directed us to Giorgio

Bassani's grave. Bassani wrote a cycle of stories, all set in Ferrara, the most famous of which is 'The Garden of the Finzi-Continis', published in 1962. This is a troubling novel, better known (but not better told) in Vittorio De Sica's film version of 1971: for the length of it the narrator pursues the beautiful, teasing Micol Finzi-Contini without success, while its deeper story is about the imprisoning of the Finzi-Contini family in the park around their grand country house, for the family is Jewish, deeply Italian in thought and ways, and the victim both of the Racial Laws enacted by Fascism in 1938 and Fascism's collaboration with the Nazis to deport Italian Jews in 1943. What if Mussolini's regime had chosen not to enact those laws? What could have been done to resist the deportation of the Jews in 1943? One can wrestle with these questions without finding definitive answers, only staring at a pool of anxiety.

Ferrara had a proud, well-established Jewish community, but 150 of them died in the death camps. Among them are Micol and her family. They are fictional, but Bassani, Jewish himself, sought to use their story to commemorate the existence of the Ferrara Jews, mixing as he does so both despair and celebration. Micol lives in the present, preferring the past even more, while "for the future, in itself, she only harboured an abhorrence". Yet Bassani signals for us the way the dead can still communicate with us, or we with them. The novel opens with a scene from after the war when the narrator visits the Etruscan necropolis of Cerveteri near Rome. These tombs are 2500 years old but he discovers that he too might care still about the Etruscans buried there. What disturbs him most therefore was that of Micol and members of her family, "no one knows whether they have any grave at all." That we still care about Bassani and his story is measured not just in the critical attention his work now receives but in the fact that his grave in Ferrara has become a site of pilgrimage. Stones on the grave indicate the numbers that make the visit to look at it.

My mind was so taken up with these sombre reflections that they quite dismissed the life-affirming vividness of events at Lord's. If I had been there at the time, my train of thought would have been on how on earth were Middlesex to take 10 wickets in 40 overs. Yet all things, it proved, were possible, and the fall of wickets was like this: 1-27, 2-39, 3-48, 4-90, 5-153, 6-160, 7-174, 8-178, 9-178, 10-178. This sequence prompts in acute ways questions of how players rouse themselves to success with either bat or ball. What did the opening batsmen tell themselves? Ditto the opening bowlers? What did Bresnan tell himself when he came in at 48 for 3? What was Gale's frame of mind as he made 22 runs, and Bressie was going well, again, at the other end? How did Rayner feel going at 6.4 and over? Or Finn at 6 an over? Do the tail-enders bat it out for a draw? Can Roland-Jones summon up his blood sufficiently to knock them over?

It was a close-run thing. To all concerned, victory to either Middlesex or Yorkshire seemed inevitable. Yet nothing is inevitable until it happens. At 160 for 6, there were 55 balls left for Middlesex to take 4 wickets. Tail-enders no longer roll over, so survival for 55 balls was surely possible. Except that was not on offer. Gale, a man of his word, wanted 80 runs off those 55. It was a juicy prospect for the bowlers, especially for Roland-Jones and Finn, two high-octane performers. Roland-Jones took Rafiq's wicket on the last ball of an over. Finn then bowled Patterson on the last ball of his next over. On the first ball of the next over, Roland-Jones bowled the redoubtable Andy Hodd. Although it was not immediately obvious, Roland-Jones was suddenly on a hat-trick. Could the man striding to the wicket be the one to deny him? Ryan Sidebottom's locks suggest he has stepped from an Attic vase, and if from an Attic vase, then he is surely the Odysseus of county cricket, "the man of many wiles, who had suffered much, who had seen much" – and who had triumphed much. What should we therefore expect? The 2015 Middlesex-Yorkshire game was not necessarily a guide, but it proved to be one since Roland-Jones had swept Yorkshire aside in their second innings with 27 for 5. In another life this might have been Ryan's moment, but not this one: with his next ball, Roland-Jones clean bowled him and Middlesex had won the match with a hat-trick. Officially it was victory by 61 runs; unofficially it was a victory by 28 balls.

No one could have known the result in advance. It did not stop everyone speculating about it, and many people predicting what they felt was likely to happen. Furthermore, betting on sports, not just horses, is now widespread, which allows sentiment to spread like smoke in the air. At the start of the day, Yorkshire were evens favourites to win, with Middlesex on 4-1 and Somerset on 11-5. By the end of the morning, Somerset had become favourites to win at 4-5 on. Then the topsy-turviness started. Unlike in a horse race where you have starting odds, and then the race is suddenly over, cricket is so drawn out that a game can turn on its head almost imperceptibly. When the declaration was made and Yorkshire were set to score 240 in 40 overs, Somerset looked out of the race. But fascinatingly Somerset started to come back. When Yorkshire was 39 for 2 at 3.41 p.m., Yorkshire drifted to third favourites and when Willey was out at 4 o'clock, leaving them needing 188 off 156 balls, Somerset were evens favourites. An hour later, when Yorkshire needed 87 runs in 60 balls, a demanding total but they still had 5 wickets in hand, Somerset were 4-5 on. They might just have been able to start raising the cup of victory to their lips.

And then Roland-Jones dashed it from them.

After our visit to the Jewish cemetery we had wandered back to our flat. I was too exhausted mentally by our sightseeing to be trembling with excitement as I opened my tablet to learn the result. The facts were there, but what was their import, their emotional charge even? Slowly a different set of feelings from the ones experienced that afternoon began to take hold of me. An immediate flavour of events was given by a series of emails from a friend who is a fervent supporter of Middlesex:

23 September, 4.59: Middlesex could still do it, come on lads . . .

5.01: Bressnan [sic] just out . . . Game on!

5.15: 6-FER: . . . into soft underbelly of Yorkshire

5.27: 8-FER: come on the 'Sex

5.27: First ball! 9 down . . .

5.29: . . . Arnie [sic] Sidebottom . . . what a season!

5.32: AND YES . . . that was a hat-trick to win it!

I had an inkling from afar at the wondrous course of events, and in the days following, especially after I had got back to the UK, I was able to gauge in more tranquillity how potent it had all been, especially at Lord's that day, but also in Taunton. The attendance figures at Lord's for the final match came to 21,595 for all four days, the highest paying attendance for a County Championship match at Lord's since May 1966, and the fourth-day crowd was 7,408. They could all say to themselves, "I was there."

Cricket, like all sport, like all history indeed, is full of 'what ifs'. The table ended up:

Middlesex   230 points

Somerset   226 points

Yorkshire   211 points

Middlesex, it turned out at the end, had been deducted 4 points for a slow over rate. Now supposing that Somerset had gathered enough points earlier in the season to end on 231 rather than 226? And that Middlesex, having got to the line with 234 points, then had 4 points deducted, so that the trophy in the act of being passed to them was suddenly placed in Somerset's grateful hands? Such delicious thoughts should not be entertained: Middlesex were unbeaten all season, winning 6 games, drawing 10, as opposed to Somerset winning 6, drawing 9 and losing one. For a neutral, it had to be Middlesex in the end.

Less praiseworthy I felt were the rumblings from other teams, which occasionally moved from the dressing room to the media, that Somerset prepared its pitches for spin as if this was not the spirit of cricket. While I was in Taunton in August, at the end of the game a Somerset supporter commented to me that he was anxious the pitch inspectors were snooping around: would Somerset be penalised for preparing an 'extreme' pitch? In the event they were not and in a way the justice of their cause was proved by their thrashing of Yorkshire with spin in the penultimate round on a pitch that would hardly have been prepared as friendly to spin. Following that game, Chris Rogers had commented wisely that Leach had been one of the chief beneficiaries of playing on more turning surfaces, but was he ready to play for England? Rogers replied: "I'm still a big believer that you need more than one good season to play for England. With Jack, I think his game's in order, I think emotionally he still has a bit of way to go and I don't think he'll be upset with me saying that." Reading this at the time (Cricinfo match report by David Hopps on 15 September 2016), I felt that Rogers's honesty was uncomplicated, admirably unspun one might say. As it turned out, Leach was, if not 'upset' with Rogers, then 'not in agreement'. In The Times of 15th November he revealed to reporter Richard Hobson, "We had an honest conversation about that interview."

At the end of the season, there was a larger context to this discussion about the place of spin in county cricket. By coincidence –

but a coincidence that takes on meaning – England were to tour Bangladesh and India, accompanied by much wailing in the press at the lack of a world-class spinner in the team. In the hothouse discussions, Leach's name got mentioned as a candidate for the tour. In the end, Moeen Ali, Adil Rashid, Zafar Ansari and Gareth Batty were the spinners chosen, while Jack Leach's career was not put in jeopardy by participation in the India tour, but instead given the chance to mature and improve by inclusion in the England Lions squad (along with Ollie Rayner, Middlesex's spin bowler). England's quest for a world-class spinner continues, and the conclusion is obvious: they are hardly likely to acquire such a hero unless spin is allowed to play a significant part in the County Championship. In this respect I felt Somerset topped the table, supplying days of spin heaven to us all.

5 EPILOGUE: THE RETURN OF TRANQUILLITY

We have all calmed down now, in Middlesex, in Yorkshire, in Taunton, certainly in neutral Norfolk. What if the two events – my private visit to the cemeteries in Ferrara and the public excitement of the eleventh-hour climax to the county season – had not coincided? It was clear that my life would have been the poorer. That it was possible to encounter these two polar opposites of human existence did not entail a cancelling out one of the other, but an affirmation that fits into our transcending of these events under the standard of eternity.

Back home, and with mind tethered firmly to the here and now, I concluded tritely that what had happened at the end of the cricket season was a victory for sport, and more excitingly a victory for long-form cricket, especially as it manifests itself every season in the County Championship. In whirlwind times, such as we live in, or seem to live in, tradition can feel as if it has gone beyond its consumption date, and it is especially prone to be killed off if it is not making enough financial return.

Questions of profit and loss underpinned cricket chatter in the 2016/17 winter regarding the impact of the proposals for a new Twenty20 competition, to be introduced in 2020 (a signal triumph for the marketing department), which will unsettle the existing Twenty20 competition, possibly unhorse the one-day competition, and discomfort the County Championship if only in further juxtaposing the raucous hyperbole of the one with the muted pleasures of the other. Since poor, catastrophic even, balance sheets can be found in a number of clubs, it is hard to make a financial argument against the proposals, but there is a cultural argument that the County Championship should be sustained. It is the form of the game from which the England Test team is drawn, and it is in that version of cricket that national identity and national pride are deeply embedded. But then subtle advocates of blast cricket will point not just to the likely financial gain to the counties from the new proposals but also to the way it is influencing long-form cricket for the better. Ben Stokes clubbed 258 runs in 198 balls, with 11 sixes, in England's game against South Africa in January 2016. His innings did not win the match, but the different tempo was compelling even to a traditionalist. Consider too players like David Warner and Joss Butler. Warner opens for Australia in all three formats. He played his first internationals in 2008/9 as a Twenty20 specialist, but when he made his Test debut in 2011, in his second match he carried his bat through the innings. Qualities of patience and guile were added to attacking ones, not that these had been jettisoned: in January 2017, playing Pakistan, he became the first Test batsmen to strike a century before lunch on the first day since Majid Khan against New Zealand in 1976. Buttler's case is slightly different. He played his first Twenty20 cricket for England in 2011, and his first one-dayers in 2012. He was part of the Test team in 2014 as a wicketkeeper-batsman, but lost his place in 2015, only to be brought back in late 2016 as a specialist batsman almost as if his explosive batting was a necessary team ingredient.

The truth is that skills learned in the short form are finding their way into the long form with the capacity of enriching that spectacle considerably. Might there not in time be a reverse movement? As players are blooded in the short form, might they not feel an itch to try their hand at the different but related skills of long-form cricket? One aspect of the brilliance of Joe Root, the new England star, is the way he flourishes currently in all three forms of the game, and has the ability, like Warner, not only to adapt to each one but to deploy lessons learned in one form to the other.

"If you love cricket, then you will love Test cricket most of all, and if you do not love Test cricket most of all, then you cannot be a true lover of cricket." That should be in the form of a question not a statement, the answer to which is delicately balanced. Perhaps in the end it is about taste, but Test cricket has an extra dimension from the way it originated and developed in this country, the way it spread through the world (if not the USA, Russia, China *et alia deserta*), and the way it feels linked to our national identity, the way we look at ourselves. Finally, it is a debate about the nature of excitement, or more philosophically, of pleasure. At the finals of the World ICC Twenty20 in April 2016 the West Indies brilliantly wrested victory from England in the final over. I followed online in California, finally sucked into a Twenty20 game, experiencing the electric frisson of excitement. For Carlos Brathwaite to hit 4 sixes in 4 balls in the final over is *magnifique, mais ce n'est pas le cricket*, surely? For pleasure, of a peculiar kind, it cannot match the slow ratcheting of tension experienced in the England v. Australia Test at Edgbaston in 2005. On the fourth day Australia went from 107 runs short of victory with only 2 wickets in hand to 3 runs short of victory all out.

If this is the case, then it remains a pressing need to find the right composition of the England Test team. One department currently remains a conundrum: how to find a world-class spinner? One answer is clear: a necessary condition, even if it is not a sufficient one, is to have spinners coming through the county ranks. Going to spin heaven in Taunton gave a glimpse of what is necessary. More soberly but more encouragingly, even if it is a boring statistic, 10,094 overs of spin were bowled in the County Championship in 2016 against 8,463 in 2015.

The County Championship is not a starry place, which is another aspect of it being out of vogue at the moment, but following performances in the County Championship does increase interest in the composition of the Test team. I discovered this in the winter, when Jack Leach was roped into the Lions tour. Suddenly I felt on the inside with that decision. But there was more: for the last two Tests against India, when England needed to find a batsmen to replace Hameed who had been so unfortunately injured, Keaton Jennings was summoned. His scores in Taunton in August were only 14 and 0, but he had captained Durham in the place of Collingwood, so clearly he had a future in long-form cricket, even at debt-ridden Durham. My picture of him was a focussed one, not the unfocussed one I would have had if I had not seen him play.

A final reason to cherish the County Championship is the pleasure it gives to spectators, not just the scattered crowds at county grounds sitting through sun, wind and rain, but those who follow their team online and on social media, and even doing so in obscure quarters of the globe. While the quantity of county supporters may feel deficient, the quality, dare one say, is of the highest. There is a link between the county and the heart. Yorkshire supporters, even those outside the county, have a connection to Yorkshire, and West Country loyalties to Somerset are among the strongest you will find. There is too a potent depth of knowledge of the history of the game among them. And there is the sheer pleasure of watching it. A month after the season end I encountered someone who at the beginning of the year had set himself the task of seeing all eighteen counties from the two divisions of the County Championship in action, and had succeeded in doing so. When I said, "What, you would attend one day of play at each game?" he replied, "Oh no! I go for the full match." I was dumbfounded at the logistics of doing this and admired profoundly his devotion.

the captains and the kings depart

6   POSTCARDS

River Tone (above) in Taunton, recipient of balls struck by mighty blows from the cricket square. Below: the Garner gates at the western end of the ground.

Somerset cricket museum is housed in an attractive stone building (left) with lancet windows on the gable end. The showroom for the batmakers Millichamp and Hall (right) is adjacent.

Taunton and Ferrara are
marked by verticality: St
Mary Magdalene in
Hammet Street (above)
and the piazza of the
Duomo, Ferrara (right)

Stained glass of 'Somersetshire Musketeer 1685' in St Mary Magdalene: swords into ploughshares, muskets into cricket bats— in a later generation, he might be a member of the Stragglers' Club.

Angels etched into the glass doors of St Mary Magdalene, no doubt trumpeting Somerset CC's achievements in 2016.

SCORECARDS

SOMERSET V DURHAM: 4-6 AUGUST 2016

Somerset 1st innings

ME Trescothick	c Borthwick b Rushworth	6
TB Abell	c Poynter b Onions	0
CJL Rogers*	c Stoneman b Coughlin	30
JC Hildreth	b Wood	34
J Allenby	c Poynter b Coughlin	11
PD Trego	b Wood	16
RE van der Merwe	c Borthwick b Wood	0
C Overton	b Rushworth	42
RC Davies†	c Stoneman b Onions	31
MJ Leach	not out	12
TD Groenewald	c Hickey b Rushworth	2
Extras		0
Total	(all out; 41.1 overs)	**184**

Fall of wickets 1-6 (Abell, 1.1 ov), 2-6 (Trescothick, 2.1 ov), 3-61 (Rogers, 12.6 ov), 4-77 (Hildreth, 17.6 ov), 5-81 (Allenby, 18.5 ov), 6-82 (van der Merwe, 19.5 ov), 7-115 (Trego, 27.1 ov), 8-166 (Davies, 36.3 ov), 9-170 (Overton, 37.5 ov), 10-184 (Groenewald, 41.1 ov)

Bowling: C Rushworth 10.1-0-47-3; G Onions 14-1-65-2; P Coughlin 10-0-48-2; MA Wood 7-1-24-3

Durham 1st innings

MD Stoneman	c Trescothick b Leach	35
KK Jennings*	c Trescothick b van der Merwe	14
SG Borthwick	c Hildreth b van der Merwe	16
MJ Richardson	c Allenby b Leach	0
SW Poynter†	c Rogers b van der Merwe	7
P Coughlin	b Overton	30
GJ Muchall	lbw b Leach	13
AJ Hickey	not out	36

MA Wood	c Allenby b Leach	27
C Rushworth	lbw b van der Merwe	0
G Onions	lbw b Leach	4
Extras		7
Total	(all out; 61.3 overs)	**189**

Fall of wickets 1-38 (Stoneman, 10.5 ov), 2-58 (Borthwick, 16.1 ov), 3-65 (Jennings, 18.3 ov), 4-69 (Richardson, 21.2 ov), 5-73 (Poynter, 28.2 ov), 6-102 (Muchall, 35.4 ov), 7-141 (Coughlin, 47.4 ov), 8-181 (Wood, 57.4 ov), 9-182 (Rushworth, 58.4 ov), 10-189 (Onions, 61.3 ov)

Bowling C Overton 11-4-30-1; TD Groenewald 4-2-14-0; J Allenby 2-0-10-0; MJ Leach 19.3-2-69-5; RE van der Merwe 25-7-59-4

Somerset 2nd innings

ME Trescothick	c Borthwick b Rushworth	0
TB Abell	c Poynter b Onions	0
CJL Rogers*	lbw b Rushworth	0
JC Hildreth	c Muchall b Onions	8
J Allenby	c Borthwick b Wood	15
PD Trego	lbw b Onions	0
RE van der Merwe	b Onions	47
C Overton	b Hickey	38
RC Davies†	c Borthwick b Hickey	49
MJ Leach	b Wood	0
TD Groenewald	not out	20
Extras		3
Total	(all out; 40.5 overs)	**180**

Fall of wickets 1-0 (Trescothick, 0.1 ov), 2-0 (Rogers, 0.5 ov), 3-0 (Abell, 1.1 ov), 4-21 (Hildreth, 7.2 ov), 5-21 (Trego, 7.5 ov), 6-33 (Allenby, 10.3 ov), 7-105 (van der Merwe, 23.5 ov), 8-117 (Overton, 28.6 ov), 9-128 (Leach, 31.2 ov), 10-180 (Davies, 40.5 ov)

Bowling C Rushworth 7-1-28-2; G Onions 14-2-50-4; MA Wood 7-0-51-2; SG Borthwick 3-0-26-0; AJ Hickey 8.5-1-19-2; P Coughlin 1-0-3-0

Durham 2nd innings

MD Stoneman	b van der Merwe	57
KK Jennings*	lbw b Overton	0
SG Borthwick	c Hildreth b Overton	9
MJ Richardson	lbw b Leach	33
GJ Muchall	c Trescothick b van der Merwe	17
SW Poynter†	lbw b Leach	12
G Onions	lbw b Leach	0
P Coughlin	c Allenby b Leach	0
AJ Hickey	not out	0
MA Wood	c Trescothick b van der Merwe	1
C Rushworth	c Allenby b van der Merwe	0
Extras		7
Total	(all out; 44.4 overs)	**136**

Fall of wickets 1-1 (Jennings, 0.5 ov), 2-19 (Borthwick, 6.3 ov), 3-88 (Richardson, 27.2 ov), 4-118 (Stoneman, 34.1 ov), 5-127 (Muchall, 36.5 ov), 6-130 (Onions, 41.5 ov), 7-130 (Coughlin, 41.6 ov), 8-135 (Poynter, 43.2 ov), 9-136 (Wood, 44.3 ov), 10-136 (Rushworth, 44.4 ov)

Bowling   C Overton   8-0-31-2;   TD Groenewald   2-0-7-0;   RE van der Merwe   17.4-3-45-4; MJ Leach   17-3-46-4

Toss – Somerset
Points – Somerset 19, Durham 3

* * *

SOMERSET V NOTTINGHAMSHIRE: 20-22 SEPTEMBER 2016

Somerset 1st innings

ME Trescothick	c Read b Ball	25
TB Abell	c Libby b Ball	8
CJL Rogers*	c Mullaney b Ball	132
JC Hildreth	c Read b Hutton	135
PD Trego	lbw b Ball	9
L Gregory	b Imran Tahir	2
RE van der Merwe	lbw b Imran Tahir	0

C Overton	c Patel b Ball	0
RC Davies†	c Mullaney b Ball	0
DM Bess	c Lumb b Patel	41
MJ Leach	not out	2
Extras		11
Total	(all out; 110.5 overs)	**365**

Fall of wickets   1-32 (Trescothick, 10.2 ov), 2-33 (Abell, 12.6 ov), 3-302 (Rogers, 84.3 ov), 4-308 (Hildreth, 85.6 ov), 5-322 (Gregory, 93.1 ov), 6-322 (Trego, 94.2 ov), 7-322 (Overton, 94.4 ov), 8-322 (van der Merwe, 95.1 ov), 9-322 (Davies, 96.4 ov), 10-365 (Bess, 110.5 ov)

Bowling   JT Ball   26-9-57-6;   BA Hutton   20-4-62-1;   Imran Tahir   22-5-92-2;   M Carter   17-2-63-0;   SR Patel   20.5-3-61-1;   SJ Mullaney   5-1-21-0

Nottinghamshire 1st innings

SJ Mullaney	c Abell b Gregory	5
JD Libby	c Abell b Bess	42
TJ Moores	c Gregory b Bess	10
MJ Lumb	c & b Bess	29
SR Patel	st Davies b Leach	12
WT Root	c Abell b Leach	10
CMW Read*†	run out (sub [MTC Waller])	4
BA Hutton	c Overton b Bess	2
M Carter	c Overton b Leach	0
JT Ball	lbw b Bess	2
Imran Tahir	not out	16
Extras		6
Total	(all out; 64.5 overs)	**138**

Fall of wickets 1-9 (Mullaney, 3.3 ov), 2-38 (Moores, 26.5 ov), 3-91 (Libby, 48.5 ov), 4-92 (Lumb, 50.3 ov), 5-108 (Patel, 55.2 ov), 6-117 (Read, 59.4 ov), 7-120 (Root, 61.4 ov), 8-120 (Carter, 61.5 ov), 9-120 (Hutton, 62.6 ov), 10-138 (Ball, 64.5 ov)

Bowling   C Overton   9-1-24-0;   L Gregory   6-3-10-1;   DM Bess 22.5-10-43-5;   MJ Leach   21-6-42-3;   RE van der Merwe   6-0-15-0

Somerset 2nd innings

ME Trescothick	c Mullaney b Carter	39
TB Abell	lbw b Hutton	10
CJL Rogers*	not out	100
RC Davies†	st Read b Patel	59
PD Trego	b Patel	55
C Overton	c Imran Tahir b Patel	21
L Gregory	not out	20
Extras		9
Total	(5 wickets dec; 57 overs)	**313**

Did not bat   RE van der Merwe, DM Bess, MJ Leach, JC Hildreth

Fall of wickets 1-30 (Abell, 7.5 ov), 2-60 (Trescothick, 16.1 ov), 3-173 (Davies, 37.2 ov), 4-251 (Trego, 47.1 ov), 5-281 (Overton, 53.2 ov)

Bowling   JT Ball 14-0-71-0; BA Hutton 8-1-38-1; SR Patel 15-1-95-3; M Carter 16-1-88-1; Imran Tahir 2-0-11-0; WT Root 2-0-5-0

Nottinghamshire 2nd innings

SJ Mullaney	c Trego b van der Merwe	18
JD Libby	run out (sub[MTC Waller])	26
TJ Moores	run out (Trego)	4
MJ Lumb	lbw b van der Merwe	31
SR Patel	lbw b Overton	37
WT Root	not out	66
CMW Read*†	lbw b Leach	0
BA Hutton	b Leach	0
M Carter	c Trescothick b van der Merwe	5
JT Ball	st Davies b Leach	11
Imran Tahir	c Trego b Leach	6
Extras		11
Total	(all out; 63.2 overs)	**215**

Fall of wickets 1-48 (Mullaney, 16.2 ov), 2-53 (Libby, 20.1 ov), 3-55 (Moores, 23.1 ov), 4-112 (Lumb, 37.2 ov), 5-138 (Patel, 44.5 ov), 6-149

(Read, 51.4 ov), 7-149 (Hutton, 51.6 ov), 8-190 (Carter, 58.2 ov), 9-207 (Ball, 61.4 ov), 10-215 (Imran Tahir, 63.2 ov)

Bowling C Overton 10-2-30-1; L Gregory 2-1-13-0; PD Trego 2-1-1-0; DM Bess 10-3-34-0; MJ Leach 21.2-5-69-4; RE van der Merwe 18-4-59-3

Toss - Somerset
Points - Somerset 23, Nottinghamshire 3

* * *

MIDDLESEX V YORKSHIRE: 20-23 SEPTEMBER 2016
Middlesex 1st innings

SD Robson	lbw b Brooks	0
NRT Gubbins	c Lyth b Bresnan	125
NRD Compton	lbw b Brooks	8
DJ Malan	b Willey	22
SS Eskinazi	b Brooks	12
JA Simpson†	lbw b Bresnan	15
JEC Franklin*	c Hodd b Bresnan	48
OP Rayner	not out	15
TS Roland-Jones	c Lyth b Brooks	7
TJ Murtagh	c Gale b Brooks	0
ST Finn	c Lyth b Brooks	6
Extras		12
Total	(all out; 108.3 overs)	**270**

Fall of wickets 1-11 (Robson, 3.4 ov), 2-33 (Compton, 11.4 ov), 3-57 (Malan, 17.2 ov), 4-97 (Eskinazi, 33.4 ov), 5-154 (Simpson, 56.6 ov), 6-229 (Gubbins, 92.2 ov), 7-244 (Franklin, 96.3 ov), 8-254 (Roland-Jones, 104.1 ov), 9-258 (Murtagh, 106.5 ov), 10-270 (Finn, 108.3 ov)

Bowling RJ Sidebottom 22-12-29-0; JA Brooks 23.3-2-65-6; DJ Willey 16-1-71-1; SA Patterson 17-9-32-0; TT Bresnan 23-7-48-3; Azeem Rafiq 7-1-15-0

Yorkshire 1st innings

A Lyth	b Finn	43
AZ Lees	b Roland-Jones	0
GS Ballance	c Rayner b Roland-Jones	0
AW Gale*	c Rayner b Roland-Jones	0
TT Bresnan	not out	142
AJ Hodd†	lbw b Roland-Jones	64
DJ Willey	lbw b Murtagh	22
Azeem Rafiq	b Murtagh	65
SA Patterson	c Rayner b Finn	11
JA Brooks	c Gubbins b Murtagh	0
RJ Sidebottom	b Rayner	23
Extras		20
Total	(all out; 116.3 overs)	**390**

Fall of wickets 1-14 (Lees, 5.4 ov), 2-32 (Ballance, 9.2 ov), 3-32 (Gale, 9.4 ov), 4-53 (Lyth, 15.6 ov), 5-169 (Hodd, 51.3 ov), 6-204 (Willey, 60.6 ov), 7-318 (Azeem Rafiq, 88.3 ov), 8-333 (Patterson, 93.5 ov), 9-334 (Brooks, 94.4 ov), 10-390 (Sidebottom, 116.3 ov)

Bowling   TJ Murtagh   32-4-96-3;   TS Roland-Jones   29-5-73-4; JEC Franklin   9-1-32-0;   ST Finn   30-4-105-2;   OP Rayner   16.3-1-70-1

Middlesex 2nd innings

NRT Gubbins	c & b Azeem Rafiq	93
SD Robson	c Lees b Sidebottom	0
NRD Compton	b Brooks	1
DJ Malan	c Brooks b Lees	116
SS Eskinazi	not out	78
JA Simpson†	b Lees	31
JEC Franklin*	c & b Lyth	30
Extras		10
Total	(6 wickets dec; 93.5 overs)	**359**

Did not bat   TS Roland-Jones, OP Rayner, ST Finn, TJ Murtagh

Fall of wickets 1-1 (Robson, 0.6 ov), 2-2 (Compton, 3.6 ov), 3-200 (Gubbins, 68.1 ov), 4-265 (Malan, 86.4 ov), 5-303 (Simpson, 88.4 ov), 6-359 (Franklin, 93.5 ov)

Bowling RJ Sidebottom 13-0-36-1; JA Brooks 15-5-48-1; TT Bresnan 12-3-33-0; SA Patterson 14-5-40-0; DJ Willey 10-3-21-0; Azeem Rafiq 18-3-46-1; A Lyth 7.5-0-77-1; AZ Lees 4-0-51-2

Yorkshire 2nd innings

A Lyth	c Robson b Roland-Jones	13
AZ Lees	c Gubbins b Murtagh	20
DJ Willey	c Eskinazi b Murtagh	11
GS Ballance	c Robson b Finn	30
TT Bresnan	lbw b Roland-Jones	55
AW Gale*	b Roland-Jones	22
AJ Hodd†	b Roland-Jones	17
Azeem Rafiq	c Simpson b Roland-Jones	4
SA Patterson	b Finn	2
JA Brooks	not out	0
RJ Sidebottom	b Roland-Jones	0
Extras		4
Total	(all out; 35.2 overs)	**178**

Fall of wickets 1-27 (Lyth, 5.6 ov), 2-39 (Lees, 10.3 ov), 3-48 (Willey, 12.4 ov), 4-98 (Ballance, 22.2 ov), 5-153 (Bresnan, 29.5 ov), 6-160 (Gale, 31.5 ov), 7-174 (Azeem Rafiq, 33.6 ov), 8-178 (Patterson, 34.6 ov), 9-178 (Hodd, 35.1 ov), 10-178 (Sidebottom, 35.2 ov)

Bowling TJ Murtagh 8-1-28-2; TS Roland-Jones 12.2-0-54-6; OP Rayner 5-0-32-0; ST Finn 10-0-60-2

Toss - Uncontested, Yorkshire elected to bowl first
Points - Middlesex 17, Yorkshire 7

SOURCES AND THANKS

First thanks must be to Josh Burrows for his piece in The Times of Saturday 24th September, 'Was declaration bowling a fair tactic?' in which he used the simile about terriers and the cat. I plagiarized this idea for a title. In the same edition of The Times, an anonymous piece headed 'Declaration, elation – how day unfolded' analysed the changing odds through the last day of the Middlesex-Yorkshire game. Andy Bull in The Guardian online (The Spin) of 4 January had a revealing piece on the decline of the draw in long-form cricket. I was grateful to the general excellence of the reporting on Cricinfo, especially the scorecards and statistics. I refer in the text to Harold Gimblett which I could not have done without David Foot's remarkable biography, 'Harold Gimblett: tormented genius of cricket', first published by Heinemann in 1982, and re-published as a Star paperback by WH Allen in 1984.

I garnered some very useful comments and advice from Charles Barr and my brother-in-law, Jack Pennell, when they read the text. My niece, Emma Roebuck, did the drawing on the title page. My wife Maggie's benign favour of the game of cricket remains a considerable source of encouragement.

The pictures were taken with a Nikon Coolpix S6400.

Tim Cawkwell, Norwich, UK

ABOUT THE AUTHOR

Tim Cawkwell was born in 1948 and lives in Norwich in the United Kingdom. He is the author of several books on film, travel and cricket:

- *The World Encyclopaedia of Film* (co-editor, 1972)
- *Film Past Film Future* (2011)
- *Temenos 2012*, a diary about the Temenos film festival in Greece in 2012
- *From Neuralgistan to the Elated kingdom: a personal journey inside Sicily* (2013)
- *Between Wee Free and Wi Fi: Scotland and the UK belong surely?* (2013)
- *The New Filmgoer's Guide to God* (2014)
- *A Tivoli Companion* (2015)
- *Cricket's Pure Pleasure: the story of an extraordinary match – Middlesex v. Yorkshire, September 2015* (2016)

In 2008 he launched his own website for writing about the cinema, www.timcawkwell.co.uk, which he has regularly maintained ever since, later adding to it a Wordpress blog, www.cawkwell200.com. In 2013 he set up his own imprint, Sforzinda Books, as an outlet for his publishing.

The tale of two terriers and the Somerset cat is his second cricket book after *Cricket's Pure Pleasure*.